Lorenz Filius

Thrusted Inspirations

Progressive thoughts into a bluish sky

© Lorenz Filius 2015

Imprint
Filius, Lorenz: Thrusted Inspirations
© Lorenz Filius, 2015
Produced and published by: BoD - Books on Demand, Norderstedt
ISBN: 978-3-7386-4541-5

Bibliographic information of the German National Library
The German National Library has registered this publication in the German National Bibliography. Detailed bibliographical information can be requested via the internet address http://dnb.d-nb.de

Table of contents

Natural inspirations   9

Outer inspirations   47

Inner inspirations   131

Preface

No understanding can be forced then; but capable of more than ending in some half-baked explanations its resources have a deeper ground. To understand by means of thinking is the first that one may think of when reflecting on content and sense, on rhyme and rhythm. Even though accompanying feelings may top deliberations off, the all in all can carry more than just a sum of inspiration, written words and found out clues: When poetry comes from one's mind, we get all that. However when it finds its way through 'heart and belly' it can hardly claim a simple one-to-one transfer of meaning or intention from one spirit to another. Sometimes not even poets can explain a one and only bottom line out of their thoughts. The magic of such poetry lies in a workaround to get a message rather than a sense: The message of Ideas that pop up in a reader's mind is then made to watch inspiring auras - instead to choose between some worked out think decisions. While facts and circumstances build up worlds and thoughts about it, the magic is a higher instance to intrude into the general infinity of opportunities.

Read and watch
what you won't find by seeing words,
which - on its own - keep visions blind.

Natural inspirations

Natural inspirations

A mindless man, 11
Wood, 11
Sirocco, 12
The mantis, 13
Where the bluster leads us, 13
Lizard's wisdom, 14
Into the doom, 14
Upon a fine line, 15
Apophis, 16
Little black hole, 17
Dandelion dream, 18
All about decay, 19
Sun in haze, 20
Dark matter, 20
Spirit's wilderness, 21
Till the last inferno, 22
The end cools down, 23
All through the light, 23
The grim reaper, 24
Sagging ground, 25
No difference of anything, 26
Chaotic order, 26
Evening tears, 27
Timeless things, 28
To where from where, 28
Just the bones, 29
Arts of ease, 30
Ditching time, 30
Atlantic, 31
The ghastly death, 32
Potential, 33
Bigger than we think, 34
An odour's spell, 35
Resistant, 36
Cuttings, 36
Taken moments, 37
Departure, 37
What nature sketched, 38
Suburbs creatures, 39
The leaves return, 40
Death Valley (Darwin), 41
Stars in water, 41
Leaving leaves, 42
Erdstall's spell, 43
Spots upon the sun, 44
Serious cat, 45
Near by my sun, 46

Natural inspirations

A mindless man

A mindless man will not expect
a passing yet before he dies;
but not for nothing he's not wise,
he stays a child in light's prospect.

Abundance boosts him time by time,
if tempted or if purified;
life is a curse if out of light,
just death is trivial in its rhyme.

Enlightenment waits in the end,
to fill the dark with scenery,
in simple objectivity,
out of the senses' tournament.

Wood

Can you see the tear on wood,
healing wounds on ancient skin,
hoary in experienced mood;
I imagine time within.

I will let it go in there,
all engulfed by rings of life,
sometimes it may lose a tear,
not to rot but to survive.

When it finally gets felled,
rather not deserving death,
maybe too much gum has welled,
still the wood can save our breath.

Natural inspirations

Sirocco

There's a hot and burning breeze,
flowing through the shadeless blue,
water rarely brings some ease,
sweat on eyebrows looks like dew.

Noon is dragging ways along,
give a lie to any aim,
not one moaning, not one song,
lethargy makes people lame.

When the evening spirit shows,
it calls up remains of vim;
heat no longer overgrows
silent thoughts of next day's dim.

Yet before it's crickets' time
to escape into the night,
bland-cool breath pervades the clime,
waiting for the morning light.

Natural inspirations

The mantis

Between the past and future's verges
there's lust in conflict with entreaty
to find out what's to come and urges;
both need to team up to be meaty.

Divinity keeps fortune's magic,
here blow of fate, there winner's blessing,
lets pray for truth, if nice, if tragic,
not treating with contempt what's pressing.

Whether to worry or to revel,
tells mantis in advance and wisely;
it won't lay tracks but our level
to let us find it out precisely.

Where the bluster leads us

In waves above horizon's line
our fate is waiting without winds;
on top, there's nothing else divine,
just questions in between give hints.

Don't bind the movement by a fence,
but give it scope to meet its form;
a little bit of reticence
may leave us calm before the storm.

The elements then find their drive,
and oceans burst the dreamy waves;
the bluster takes us through our life
until another dream it craves.

Natural inspirations

Lizard's wisdom

Watch, the lizard's watching you,
spreading magic just by chance,
shapes and colours may come true;
it's your future in advance.

As its eyebeam meets your soul,
you have watched it yet too long;
you can set tomorrow's goal,
but the lizard's wisdom's strong.

Easy to ignore your fate;
when it hurts, avert your gaze,
maybe it is not too late,
though you've lost a moment's chase.

Into the doom

Look ahead into the doom,
there's a little floating light,
brightening horizon's site;
where we go there'll be no gloom.

Here it's peaceful in the dark,
lean on, let us fall asleep,
swarming feelings take us deep;
upon welfare they'll embark.

Now and then there is a wink,
leading us to lights ahead,
heading home we lose our tread;
we leave back what faces think.

Natural inspirations

Upon a fine line

Upon a fine line we are winged,
and bound by all our life instinct,
our way seems fairly save and sealed,
our future is not yet revealed.

We're simply teased by what we are,
all by ourselves, the world is far;
what ever gave us clues and hints,
it's destiny, which always wins.

We're dancing now around our love,
and find the heavens high above;
we realize our given urge
as natural consent to merge.

Involuntarily we pause,
as if we'd wonder 'bout our cause;
and soon our senses get a sign
when poising on another line.

Natural inspirations

Apophis

Through the keyhole it will come,
opening the gate of skies,
revelation beats the drum;
what's to come is more than wise.

It's a God of ancient times,
takes its darkness into light,
leaving shadows to dead climes,
flesh burns out to stone-cold night.

Vastnesses remain unfazed,
they predestine star by star,
children's thrones are doomed when placed;
Gods are lurking from afar.

It's no everlasting fight,
just unfathomable spell;
darkness may be lit by light,
but its end is hard to tell.

Natural inspirations

Little black hole

Gazing at a little spot,
deeper as a deep sleep phase,
shapes get lost in daylight's lot,
and my field of view skews space.

No direction keeps its course,
and a helix wipes all out,
up side down - what comes, what was,
but my inner core's still stout.

All around my crutch gets loose,
there my weakness fades to naught,
cold, my breath - I feel abstruse,
hardly real what could be thought.

Senses twist around brain's hub,
and my mind's beyond each goal,
but before it's swallowed up,
I blow out that small black hole.

Natural inspirations

Dandelion dream

Just a glimpse has caught my sight
as there nothing's worked my mind,
hard to place that foreign might;
dreamland of a different kind.

That aware I've never been,
at the same time without dread,
starry flickering backs the scene,
sun on water sways my head.

Dimmed out shades leave space for more,
which that limelight may imbue;
what plain shine cannot adore,
bright transparency can do.

Then this glimpse the moment slows
draws attention to a bloom,
filigree, a blow ball shows;
life is more than we assume.

When bright yellow floods the spring,
beauty's greatness will have won
'til a tiny little thing -
dandelion's seed - flies on.

Natural inspirations

All about decay

Decay - is making things go on,
it - overlooked - affects no one;
and in a distance, something new,
too close to keep our lame poise true.

Decay - is blurring our sight,
the faded things don't shade what's wide;
diffuse it is, so safe ahead,
although it's soon or later dead.

Decay - gets finally all solved,
like heal and harm all is revolved;
disclosing death and run of life,
no wedge between these both to drive.

Decay - decaying on its own,
not scary, flesh that leaves its bone;
some anxiety in what's to come:
Decay in anger beats hell's drum.

Natural inspirations

Sun in haze

Under domes of white and grey
time is rolling all its way,
moves no shadows and no light,
takes my eyebeam out of sight.

But a shining knob-like spot
tempts a little growing dot;
flashing through my fading face,
makes it follow through the haze.

Dark matter

What we just guess,
is slipping as the biggest rest
through meshes,
dark in inexplicability,
leaving webs of sciences
a simple grid

'till

our know-how's mess,
which plagues us like a minding pest
when putting clashes
deep in truth-like abysses to see,
bursts into defiances
that minds can't fit.

Natural inspirations

Spirit's wilderness

And the snow is falling on,
where the tiger swallows men;
no companion gets along
to give life what prayers can.

And the spirits of the forms
cannot flee their wilderness;
dynasties have had their storms,
influencing timelessness.

And the river will not quake
when the winds blow heavily
since life has no higher stake
than to live without to flee.

And while fate is found and lost,
time is out of tiger's class;
tear and smile are tempest-tossed,
in between it comes to pass.

Natural inspirations

Till the last inferno

Rain is falling quietly,
silently it covers graves;
sun's inferno once will be
melting ground and what it saves.

That what happened feeds the past,
memories are weary bliss;
but a bit we make them last,
our tomorrow they may kiss.

We don't show the certitude
what we may expect from it;
future's many days to suit
dreams, which let us intuit.

So we simply take some light
to expand the dark around;
reasoned questions every night
come from answers to be found.

Natural inspirations

The end cools down

That open maw returns no call,
no being in the absent rot,
the tongue is sick to death of all,
remaining in post-mortem clot.

I search imagination's truth
for beauty and its dauntless past,
which needed to deface its youth;
we hope, but purposes won't last.

Our life in dirt seems tidy, though,
and carries nature to extremes;
the end cools down each afterglow,
those who know better lose their dreams.

All through the light

All through the light we're dancing on,
the stage of life is our world,
we don't need more to get along,
no unasked glut to get unfurled.

No dark conceit may join us now,
it's life that shines and makes us shine,
we end tomorrow anyhow,
today I'm yours and you are mine.

Natural inspirations

The grim reaper

The land has found the grim reaper,
and paradise is overseas;
but even there he's death's keeper,
he takes whatever hope may ease.

His face is covered by a hood
and catches eyesight that is doomed;
to find himself there, is no good
since he reflects what once has bloomed.

The grim reaper calls all his own,
takes one or many when he calls;
they follow him around his throne,
he taps as well as he befalls.

So be aware, once he'll be there
although he may not nod at you;
his scythe is always anywhere
and hits when you don't think it's true'.

Natural inspirations

Sagging ground

Sagging ground, a screech owl cries,
I look back, it reeks of death,
earthy smell keeps stinky breath,
seemingly about to rise.

Underground the blessing breaks,
and a bunch of flowers wilts;
as the gravestone slowly tilts,
something, cursing, now awakes.

As I slew the lantern's light,
darkness swallows all its glow,
hits a face's ghastly show,
bones are grabbing at my fright.

Then it moans and grunts at me,
out of flesh that's soaked by ground,
suddenly there's no more sound,
as all mildew is set free.

Still, I'm feeling sick and leave,
and my lantern heads for dawn,
one look back, the hunting's gone,
and the grave succumbs to grief.

Natural inspirations

No difference of anything

They make no difference to me,
the ways beyond my final way;
if coffin's rot, if spread on sea,
remains are free and no one's prey.

'Cause this is all that stays somewhere
and untouched by old times of breath;
my flesh has left my fallow sphere,
which only comforts rests of death.

However, feast on it, live on,
as I have done it now and then;
concede each other, when I'm gone,
that this and that belong to man.

Chaotic order

In chaos, nothing in its way,
at crossings, plank by plank to stay;
yet, freedom's going on so far,
but caught, whatever caused a scar.

The meshes spread, as they get chased,
what starts is always somehow based;
and in the end it looks for sense
since even this is likewise tense.

High density makes logic track,
its context - numb - it can't look back;
and chaos seems to rest in peace,
the things arrange what we can't grease.

Natural inspirations

Evening tears

Look into the evening's tears,
which were gathered by its day;
nightly dew keeps longing fears,
leaf by leaf, a fortune's way.

Once, all laughter's almost died,
there's no child that needs to cry;
all these drops are heirs of light,
otherwise no time would fly.

'Cause the heavens shine alone
until they diverge again;
who can see what stars may own,
if not we, together then.

Even if the first one's gone
and the last one yet to come,
nothing of it all is won
since each part reveals the sum.

Look into the evening lights,
look outside, along the world,
see your face in other sights,
taking part, no eyebrows furled.

Natural inspirations

Timeless things

Moments that a raindrop saves,
narrow, more than instant blinks,
send from pictures see-through waves,
cutting time in timeless things.

Stillness loses what it is,
searches streams to find its flow,
gets a meaning senses miss,
letting true confessions go.

Situatedness returns,
recollects to move the day,
courage then no longer yearns,
getting bound to thereness' way.

To where from where

The sphere is plain, and so its death,
an ocean with no soul or breath;
a pulse by God or accident
initiates a waving trend.

It takes the news across the sea,
encircling its own gravity,
its factional dispute goes round:
Is there an endpoint to be found?

It meets itself, and after all,
jumps almost off, but needs to fall,
again it must traverse the sphere
believing in 'from here to where'.

Natural inspirations

Just the bones

It leaves us just the bones,
the branches of the dead,
the roots lie under stones,
the ground gets moved ahead.

Who are we now and here
that we may ask for more?
The answer seems so clear,
on top of life's galore.

A breeze that strokes a face,
from old erosive storms,
prefigures time and place
of temporary worms.

We moulder, bottom up,
with minds on rampant growth,
but each initial hub
saves something of them both.

Natural inspirations

Arts of ease

Mist imbues remaining colour,
nests of nature keep them warm,
all succumbs to magic pallor,
takes the view out of its form.

Light surrenders facts and fiction,
truth is being made of dreams,
what we see is no addiction,
what we feel may follow streams.

Memories fade to distant summers,
let us leave their time in peace,
jumping life slinks on in mummers,
shadows show us arts of ease.

Ditching time

Time is rushing on ahead
yet before it comes to pass,
when we catch it up, it's dead,
ignorantly ditching us.

Atlantic

In the middle of no time
there's an arch of cloudless light,
spreads the world into one clime,
keeps the senses off their sight.

Calculations come to naught,
future comes from everywhere,
will not stay and can't be caught,
voices meet and disappear.

That's a moment's freest play,
all the world around's dispersed,
then the point gets torn away;
life speeds on as if rehearsed.

'Is the target a begin
and the start a prior aim?'
are those questions made to win,
forcing space in time shift's claim.

Either way, if day or night,
in the point to anywhere
life needs seemingly no might,
which pretends to need life there.

Natural inspirations

The ghastly death

Death throws gravel in our face,
tells off fortune's wandering sand,
it compels bones without grace
when inventing flesh to stand.

Death does not consider life,
it adores what memories write,
thrusts in hearts its one-way-knife,
with emotions, side by side ...

... but if trivialized or churched,
it's not more than we define;
by its brashness we get urged,
cutting life of its decline.

Send death packing, and you'll find
there's no heaven's boon to cope;
death is just a window's blind
that the living need to hope.

Potential

Light seems so lost in deepest space,
its work, unfounded in the end;
but darkness can't absorb its place,
cause light is that what darkness sent.

All jubilations' burden streams
from blackness to infinity;
gets lost in lit up holes of dreams
until it finds real potency.

Then it seems caught by clever minds,
in terms of conscious thoughts and stance;
the one and only of all science,
once preattentive, takes a chance.

It soon awakens everywhere,
chummed up in self-experience,
reflection needs someone to care,
and life can gain its relevance.

And finally the brightest light,
which instinct's genesis foresaw,
may dance in front of blackness' might,
refracting in its natural law.

If purpose, accident or more,
it needs to vanish finally;
although extinct, it leaves a spoor,
a footprint of divinity.

Natural inspirations

Bigger than we think

It is much bigger than we think,
than dreams can ever take from truth;
we laugh or cry from link to link,
but just to find our way to soothe.

It keeps much more than ever was,
and even that what comes is less;
since there's a loss of heaven's force
by frictions of our life's progress.

It's capable and it will do,
the question is not when and where;
all past and future will come true,
diverging in its central sphere.

It is, it keeps, it can itself,
not feeling lonely all along;
the ones who search it only delve,
the ones who ask may be among.

Natural inspirations

An odour's spell

An odour's spell waves peace of silence
deep in summer's evenfall,
and in between old souls foregather,
faint nostalgia they recall.
Now whispering they unfold those stories,
take the evening to their time,
we delve into some flair of comfort,
senses share a vintage chime.

They tell of love and hate and fortune,
wistfully they breathe their past,
in faded voices we find heartache,
providence lets good times last.
Embedded in romantic ruffles
memories in their blooms revive,
and tenderness of stroking pallor
gives free rein to all their life.

The giggle in the summer gardens
follows calls across the land,
but wanderlust is homeland's freedom,
and the homeland holds the band.
The generation's conversation
fades away in sunset's red,
their faces lead esteem in portraits
or in diaries of the dead.

Unreal chimes of bells are sounding,
yet a children's song by night,
the symphonies in timeless distance
save the artist's reserved pride.
Another moment in this musing,
wherein lavender smells on,
and then a sun takes us to longings
that at sunrise will be gone.

Natural inspirations

Resistant

And so we are existent
when dropped out of reality;
we're lost in time's motility,
our moment's not resistant.

The claims we live dissemble,
abduct our life to 'just to be';
still lone, when there allegedly,
each truth leaves space to ramble.

And soon we'll have departed,
all gets withdrawn by honesty,
no cut, no saving memory;
what is goes on as darted.

Cuttings

Cuttings urge the woods,
people search for death,
'lust for living' hoots,
cold as winter's breath.

Keels dig ditch by ditch,
filling them with foam;
filthy wave peaks bleach
dreams that have no poem.

Arrows split the air,   People leave their lands,
rifts distort the winds;   haunted by new worlds,
weathers in despair   no one understands
'till our crying dins.   why no peace unfurls.

Natural inspirations

Taken moments

The rains have ended in a drop,
no time that takes it from its top,
it balances what I expect
and gives slow motion scope to act.

When drops fall down, tomorrow comes
while moment's mirror halts the drums,
may lead my thoughts from heart to soul,
I lose them and the drop will roll.

Departure

Soon it is departure time,
destination no-man's-land;
fading of the church bells' chime
lays the soul in guardian's hand.

Travelling on, the wings of trust,
peace of mankind will survive;
those who stay must cope the past,
but all future saves their life.

Natural inspirations

What nature sketched

When beauty finds a silent place,
it lets us sink into its space,
our point of view becomes detached,
takes part in that what nature sketched.

There's nothing left to know or guess,
no inconvenience might stress;
the joint of mind and body's linked
to some original instinct.

We float, are moved by random drifts,
no quest directs, no purpose shifts;
the centre always gets us back,
no claim around that needs a track.

When getting almost too ideal,
a pleasant shiver's all we feel;
that is the point of our return,
a hint of what we lifelong yearn.

The scene is gone, our mood's with us,
and silence streams along our buzz;
while beauty's still and everywhere,
we brood too much and can't be there.

Natural inspirations

Suburb's creatures

Another bloodline perishes in vain,
somewhere inside, the core of city's rush,
a pet tells fellow species its pain,
they take it to the suburbs' creatures' hush.

The gap will soon be filled with human flesh
as long as it finds pulp and clueless cheese;
a devastating tone in ears and cash,
a tinnitus the world loves in decease.

Some couples still may find their tenderness,
but they are slaves of understanding's greed;
infertile, almost oversexed and genderless,
they keep new childhood chance from future's need.

Beyond, some foxes learn to read a book,
while doves take trains to pick up food downtown,
the grubs of bugs are home and dry to look
how rats wear glasses with a smart man's frown.

Natural inspirations

The leaves return

Finally the leaves return
in a moment as we yearn;
intermediate delay
is a case of yesterday.

Attitude to yawn and moan,
made by our fight alone,
since we took as given chance
each temptation in advance.

Climes and climate rearrange
what we thought to need and change;
anyway the wounds will heal,
but without our mental drill.

So the ways will stay apart,
we don't learn of nature's art;
all we know comes much too late,
our cries won't change our fate.

Natural inspirations

Death Valley (Darwin)

Eccentric relativity,
thrown out of joint, the way to be,
the human mind is pulled by grounds,
digresses humanly in rounds.

One flesh on spineless, desert clime,
averted peacefully from time,
its silence doesn't claim remorse,
what happened stays with fortune's course.

Stars in water

Stars are blinking from the lake,
swooning over sunny days,
shadows keep what lights can't take,
giving twinkling magic space.

Here from wave to wave they leap,
there a breeze takes them along,
they embed the swans that sleep,
heads in wings, they dream among.

Take my mind to distant sights,
feel like following their flow,
thoughts are long since part of lights
far ahead the old day's glow.

Soon they'll fade into the dark,
like a billion times before,
mirrored under heavens arc
till a new sun plays once more.

Natural inspirations

Leaving leaves

Watch them flying leaves ahead,
like our dreams disperse with ease;
yet tomorrow grey and dead
while today still save in trees.

Maybe life must float away,
but the rooted days stay deep;
grew around the words to say,
branching out in questions' heap:

Can a moment still be true
even if we disappear;
may young sprouts then find anew
what we were in our flair?

Like them leaving leaves, just go,
I'll be standing by your side,
where they fly we do not know,
coming back when we have died.

Natural inspirations

Erdstall's spell

Rumour's, deep in erdstall's spell,
cover times of history well,
aren't revealed to facts and figures;
past and presence real time triggers,
just a longing eye might dwell.

Gleams of hope engender fright,
feeding gloom of night mare's night
to find purchase on the quiver;
death and devils need to shiver,
hell stud, mare of heaven's might.

Life in boltholes stands in awe,
lungs feel crushed by horror's claw.
Are there humans who ain't brutish?
Oh, dear Gods, make worries vanish,
let's believe in what we draw.

As the goose-flash fades away,
and the bats have gone astray,
deathly silence swallows secrets,
leaving thoughts in empty squat pits,
no attention left to pay.

Natural inspirations

Spots upon the sun

Secret spots upon the sun,
outshined by its brightest light,
won't affect life's joy and fun;
harmless they are out of sight.

Science finds them here and there,
then they're done and had their time;
but what happened goes somewhere,
time keeps space but changes clime.

So the bloom of light stays keen,
while below it seethes on;
still audaciously serene,
nothing bears on anyone.

Once the glow will eat all mood,
when distended by its might;
secret murmur finds it rude,
ending up in peaceful night.

Time reliably wipes out
fires of colossal size;
giants, red and ugly loud,
turn into a dwarf of ice.

Natural inspirations

Serious cat

A loner, sensitive and still,
on paw steps that disguise his will,
the smoothest shadow night can get,
the ownness of a serious cat.

It roams its hunting grounds in peace,
at moment's notice it may freeze;
it stands by its familiar way
when alternating fight and play.

Once it has fixed its gaze on you,
it won't reveal its point of view;
'don't touch' is almost always law,
except you may respect the claw.

In times of sleep's intimacy
its cuddly attitudes squirm free;
enjoy when ruffling kitty's fur -
against the gain, you'll goad its purr.

Natural inspirations

Near by my sun

Near by my sun and in an idyll of the past
I lay in bliss and I was wishing it would last.
But did I ever face the chance of more,
foretelling me the truth of dust,
which covered worlds I hardly could adore?
Near by my sun and in an idyll of the past
I lay in bliss and I was wishing it would last.

Outer inspirations

Outer inspirations

In deepest sorrow, 51
The wow-signal, 53
Death is awake, 54
Over ruins, 56
Burning fast away, 58
Lame walk, 59
Backyard longing, 61
Insanity romance, 63
Falling star, 64
The ticker, 65
What kind of end, 66
Fading trains, 67
Infinite, 68
Rise and fall, 70
Beyond the core, 71
What becomes of memories, 73
Nothing happens anymore, 75
Faux pas, 77
Without commitment, 78
Black holes in our head, 80
What's the stake, 82
View resistance, 84
Out of 404, 85
Scrutinized future, 87
In rumour's place, 89
Merchandized pain, 90
Stalker, 91
Gliese 581g, 92
Brain death genius, 93
Another factory day, 94

Snob's gallop, 52
A fool's licence, 53
The very last man, 55
Jiggery-Pokery, 57
Political circle, 59
The creeping, 60
Cronyism, 62
The thinker, 64
The dead float on, 65
Pathos of progress, 66
Black on white, 67
A heart in the wall, 68
Trendy, 69
Eerie brains, 71
Diva, 72
Falling masks, 74
Sold fate, 76
Gone without an end, 77
Whiningly cold-blooded, 79
Distorting world, 81
Off the stage, 83
On screen hubbub, 84
Conquered, 86
Politically messed up, 88
Ghosts and spirits, 89
Spoiled words, 90
Last writing people, 92
Wolf in sheep's clothing, 93
Media hyped catastrophes, 94
The runner, 95

Outer inspirations (cont'd)

The shrink, 96
Burping joy, 98
End time Advent, 100
What we should fear, 101
Narcissism, 103
Heap of meat, 105
Pirates, 107
Balance of inhumanity, 109
Pages in an empty book, 110
Washed out towels, 112
Longing's sore, 113
Characters alive, 115
Sunday walk, 116
Room four hundred four, 118
Bewitched, 120
Stretched smile, 122
Famous clues, 124
Bound and pained, 126
Shine on for the child, 128
Heart's blood, 130

Inner beast, 97
Spoiled time, 99
My starlight's rising, 101
The golden age, 102
Just a cloud, 104
Village funfair, 106
Secrets, 108
Where the wind blows, 110
Majestic sledge, 111
Time frames, 112
Nobody, 114
Waste or value, 115
Contradiction's destiny, 117
Cold turkey, 119
Blind followers, 121
Lobbyism, 123
Poverty itself, 125
State of the art, 127
The wannabe writer, 129

Outer inspirations

In deepest sorrow

The world in deepest sorrow
when celebrities get flu,
the world in deepest sorrow
for a panda in the zoo,
the world in deepest sorrow
for conceited cry and hue,
the world in deepest sorrow
reads the paper on the loo.

The money all must borrow
presses words to make them true,
the money all must borrow
pays some fees to burke each clue,
the money all must borrow
sells refurbished thoughts as new,
the money all must borrow
rhymes with sorrow's askew due.

Outer inspirations

Snob's gallop

Arrogance on winds of sheen
when on horseback flying high;
no more trotting in between
people who just live and try.

Once, he sweeps across the place,
no conjuncture makes him stop,
and the rider needs his grace;
stumbling gallop moves the snob.

Watch, how fast he's out of sight,
over villages and towns,
leaving lights below his ride,
nothing over him that crowns.

Later he may halt his run,
much too easy time went on,
haggardly he claims the sun,
wondering why the dark has won.

Insecure, he jokes and laughs,
there's some pain, he won't admit,
eagerness turns to piaffes,
then he silly smiles to quit.

Outer inspirations

The wow-signal

A billion signals
we receive;
the vastness prickles,
we believe;
a moments movement,
just a POW ...
belief's improvement,
we cry wow!

A billion signals
we believe;
the vastness prickles,
we receive
a moment's movement,
we cry wow;
belief's improvement:
Let's say POW! ...

A fool's licence

Sometimes dark authorities
let the crowd disturb our peace
to provide dull minds with ease
when oppressions may displease.

Even fools know what to do,
making fun out of their woe,
but their apers without clue
cry for pain they're living through.

Outer inspirations

Death is awake

Death is dancing round our tired heads,
sounds conspired what is taking place,
just by purpose or by real threads,
who might know, who might believe the daze.

While the good won't fight for any might,
all the bad is better when it grins,
yet endangerment is out of sight,
sense gets mad and well done nonsense wins.

Panic creeps through our illusive brains
while our hearts sink to our slippery boots;
wealthy greediness lives off compliance,
made by fear that such threadbareness loots.

Finally we're dull enough and rage,
after staggering through brainwashed thoughts,
go berserk in quarantines fools' cage,
getting blood-bathed by surveillance-lords.

Then there's silence, death is waking on,
holding self-insurance well at bay.
None of us is safe, so what is won?
Victims of hysteria should pray.

Outer inspirations

The very last man

Who'll be the last man finally?
Who is it, who must die alone?
When will he live insanity,
when is the day he can't postpone?

How does he pass away with all?
No profit was intense like this.
Can knowledge matter when we fall?
A billion years keep what it is.

Old loneliness of space expands
into an unattended age;
light melts forgotten elements,
they can't escape their period's cage.

The last man maybe asks his death:
What would I find if I lived on?
There is no goal of fire's wrath,
the question is, what cold has won.

Outer inspirations

Over ruins

Over ruins of old worlds,
times grow rampant time by time;
death and pain decay in whirls
to forgive the changing clime.

Leaves and grasses overshade
ground and traces ground has won;
overgrowing culture's glade,
underneath the rats move on.

Far away from ancient towns,
modern cities keep new might;
how they think it was astounds,
they mistake it over night.

Once the newish walls will break,
being ruins in the wild;
then no hand is there to take
by a flower picking child.

Outer inspirations

Jiggery-Pokery

There they go to lose their heart
to the big auspiciousness,
glorified by fortune's bliss,
slyly looking for their part.

Their obsession is well spurred,
and their legs feel featherweight,
earlier no role they played,
now they won't be overheard.

Ways below go soon astray,
'smoke and mirrors' overhead,
dedication drives them mad,
taking to what they can't pay.

Empty paths approach their aim,
which high flyers do not share;
in their verve too unaware,
they bounce back to no one's fame.

Outer inspirations

Burning fast away

The world is burning fast away
in corners, underpinning ends;
and in between we sit and play,
just hoping what our will pretends.

Some far infernos could be seen,
extinguished wars in talking hearts;
good usualness makes solace keen
till bitter victory casts the parts.

The flares surround our peace of doubts,
are glistening reflections, though;
too much in it blows different clouds
to find the menace on the go.

Persistent mediocrity
takes happenings beyond our scenes;
we fade them out familiarly
when zapping news on TV screens.

When fires finally find us,
then malice won't knock at the door;
it wipes the curse from good men's buzz,
not granting rights to ask 'what for'.

Outer inspirations

Political circle

Sitting around the table now,
doing nothing with their eyes,
moved, on chairs, by voices, wise,
coffee's fresh, full of know how.

Then the circle saves its sphere
by the same old soothing words,
they hysterically end in flirts,
'till all know that they are there.

Fading silently in peace,
sentences don't dare to act;
sighs for free top off the fact
on the tips of tongues to please.

Lame walk

Sometimes that what's going on,
find's itself in answer's hub;
sometimes questions won't be gone
if they leave a rooty stub.

Often progress without talk
keeps the good of inner peace;
asking on, it leaves lame walk,
being beaten by will's ease.

Outer inspirations

The creeping

They're crawling on in peace,
many, many, day by day;
they forcefully decease,
gutless, gutless, without say.

They do what they may do,
but their wage comes without smile;
they cram a chosen few
when they scuff their own profile.

They need no friends, no foes,
many, many, just for bread;
in destiny's old shoes,
walking on their traceless tread.

The languor still lives on,
never satisfied by brains;
and scorn, they all have won,
makes them laugh in their restraints.

No money to be blamed,
doing what it is made for;
but those who are unnamed
jointly could have done much more.

They're creeping still along,
only living on the fly;
not worse becomes what's wrong,
those who don't stand up may lie.

Backyard longing

Below an early dusk, beyond the roofs' horizon,
the greedy, glaring sun lets backyards be agape
with copious longing, looking for a piece of sky
in the cold blue of a puddle.

The day therein is hungry for experienced time
while taking beings through their rounds,
from human life to flight instinct,
from common sense to cry of madness;
and in between the spat of feeble children
praises courage to get old.

The starry night, too high,
pours murky darkness
down the TV-consoled window rows,
feeding someone's swearing anger
with the city's poisoned silence.

I stick my head into this pull,
tearing at my bulkiness
in pressing walls around me,
and patience of my heart gets almost ripped apart,
not asking anymore:

Where is a stream that takes my thoughts along,
out of the buildings' depth,
throughout the puddles,
into an ocean of the day,
towards its cooling morning shores,
like balmy evening beaches,
which still may warm my dreams.

Outer inspirations

Cronyism

Marvellous you are,
if not, at least how you pretend,
while all our faithless praise
is teasing yours,
closing eyes to disillusion.

Come to us, don't bar your lot,
in which our peace we send;
where subtle feelings base
on yes-man's course
into cronyism's fusion.

Outer inspirations

Insanity romance

A sick mind's big insanity
adores strange romance in its act,
and victim's fright sets feelings free,
transfigured gazes make a pact.

Weird laughter meets despairing cries,
obsessively implores: Just we!
It's lust to kill in love disguise,
unsympathetic empathy.

Illusive silence, breeding harm,
not finding ways out of the scene;
an anxious breath is hard to calm
when almost choked by moron's spleen.

A nightmare thrills the atmosphere,
pulsating veins are soaked by sweat;
who'll see still beauty in blue fear,
bizarre deliciousness drives mad.

Where does this craze take longings to,
here greed for more, there urge to bolt;
what sicko shine of eyes may brew,
a dance of death will soon leave cold.

It's done, the deed is lost in peace,
the perpetrator finds some rest,
he lays a smile into the ease,
until it puts him to the test.

Outer inspirations

The thinker

He's looked at, grinned at or ignored,
they stay a while and then get bored.
Is someone there who thinks of him
when passed by into day-life's dim?

A unicum amongst the crowd,
not showing why he isn't loud,
a tender spot in routines' light,
suspicious, strange, soon out of sight.

A thought gets lost, he glances up,
a moment, made to kiss his cup,
a smile he leaves may find a smile,
it understands him for a while.

Falling star

A falling star stays all alone,
and clouds confirm its fate beyond,
there's nothing else upon its throne
but waiting darkness to respond.

An almost endless fear resumes,
what is to come when nothing goes,
another light of conscience looms
in signs of hope, which it outgrows.

It's always something going on,
despite the evidence of naught,
a star gets born, since all is won
as long as instants meet a thought.

Outer inspirations

The dead float on

May never ending peace engross,
beyond the earthly, final cross,
what big belief has kept before;
its end is like an ocean's shore.

The living stay and wave farewell,
the dead float on, their memories dwell,
the sunset in peculiar light
makes way for ways with no more fight.

No island out there in the myth,
no matter looms to struggle with,
the depth contains infinity,
what nothing else might mean to be.

Where skies meet waters in the end,
no time is left that shall be spent,
but time enough to wait for more
to reach another waiting shore.

The ticker

Tick-over lets the ticker tick,
it almost ticks away with us,
our life just ends like candle's wick:
What will remain of worked-out fuss?

But when the ticker ticks through thoughts
that casually get in its way,
it's found something to tick towards
inviting sparks of life to stay.

Outer inspirations

Pathos of progress

Where has it gone,
the pathos of our own progress?
Just dragging on,
a rest of drive that won't impress.
The spinning sense,
not feeling what it actually means,
just time it spends
when driven by on what it leans.

A feeling will,
poor imitation of the feel,
is spirit's thrill,
in tow of other people's deal.
Dull mastery
of minds before they disappear,
bores history,
because they have been never there.

What kind of end

Will there be a last remaining man,
or a being, doing what it can?
Who will be the beast with human rights,
barely understanding why it fights?

Will the final questions still be asked
when reality is no more masked?
When will all the final days begin
still containing clues what we'll have been?

Outer inspirations

Black on white

What today in black on white and page by page
I may hold in feeling hands,
will tomorrow be all right, won't leave time's stage;
edits change no written stance.

When tomorrow I get old with what I know,
finding still what's written then,
digital is what I'm told by edit's flow
in despair to change past's plan.

Constant truth is a behest of figures' fact
and forever as it is.
All that puts it to the test, leaves it uncracked
either way, what was, what is.

Fading trains

Listen to the fading trains
there's no traveller who remains,
stations, like deserted towns,
clock-hands send home drunken clowns.

Time stands still, just for a while,
neon light from tile to tile.
Is there anything that moves?
Must be shadows silence spoofs.

From afar a rumbling then,
wipes a moment schedule's ban;
soon there will be future time
which continues past times' rhyme.

Outer inspirations

A heart in the wall

A young, young heart there in the wall,
can hardly loosen stones with beats,
remorselessly no brick will fall,
a silhouette soul no daylight feeds.

Its shadow seems so castaway,
gets bypassed by the wandering sun,
and even holes of rats may play
with light through which the rats may run.

Then there's weird silence in this quiet,
expects no pitying applause,
out of the wall into our sight
the shadow falls, diverts our course.

Infinite

You
are yet
extremely small
and there a bit imposing
with your senses diving in infinity
to feel what was in closing
as one of all
is that
true

Outer inspirations

Trendy

The youngster's world is trendy,
and playing are the clones,
while bullies' social envy
sprays blood on mobile phones.

Audacity wants fainting
to feel what's going on,
a coolness that is tainting,
until one's breath is gone.

The tunnel hosts a sniffer,
no clue if life may last;
while solvents make him shiver,
the train comes much too fast.

They pee themselves when joking
as coolest wannabes;
sexism they're provoking,
not guessing whom they please.

Technology for bad boys,
print out a 3d-gun,
a barrel made by mad toys,
is loaded - oops - no fun.

When young <u>we</u> conquered meadows,
and forests made to roam,
behind the trees no shadows,
and evenings took us home.

Outer inspirations

Rise and fall

Imagine, what once happened here,
a stone by stone created sphere,
an empty space becomes life's hall,
someone puts papers on the wall.

The brick shell gets an outside then,
by brushstrokes of a busy man,
day in day out the windows shine,
the door keeps counted days in line.

And sheltered, hush, there's someone else,
two hearts can make what future tells,
the fireplace may warm their rest,
the chimney gives the stork a nest.

The years go by and leave their trace,
a child on green, around this place,
while on a bench, just arm in arm,
near by the house, two thank day's charm.

All blossoms go but will come back,
those sunny days some rain won't wreck,
however time leaves much to live,
the youngsters use what aged ones give.

One stays alone, the die is cast,
the bench invites to wine and past,
and wrinkles draw through face and home,
mature, the grass where weed may roam.

And now and then a grandchild cares,
it listens to forgetful tears,
gets this and that from quiet talk,
and helps the tired heart to walk.

A smile meets finally the dusk,
no question left horizons ask,
tomorrow breaks the windows' glass,
tonight, behind them one will pass.

Outer inspirations

Eerie brains

So eerily some brains are raving,
primeval soup is what they're craving,
in bubbles they are pulling strings,
pulsating cells will force bad things.

They pin their hopes on membrane's quiver,
these simply grow along our shiver,
and when new DNA gets strong,
some RNA will get it wrong.

Such code of handicraft genetics
must lack each sense beyond weird ethics,
and monster mania makes them blind,
eroding finally our mind.

Beyond the core

In centre's orbit there's a point,
which sees itself too much as core;
although it claims a central joint,
it gets rejected as before.

The point increases its progress
by getting faster furiously;
centrifugally moods access
the point to ban it instantly.

And so it overstates the case,
concluding reasons much too late;
to claim the centre of a place,
is not what circle's may debate.

Outer inspirations

Diva

She swooshes and defends her fame,
her talent gals her passionate name,
is talked of yet before she talks,
and snootily applause she stalks.

Then gifted, she is what she can,
no doubt, if woman or if man,
but art itself can't make her proud
until it's out of line and loud.

A puppet out of fantasy,
an egomaniac's remedy;
when outgrowing the inner bloke,
it may romance the outer joke.

The view is changing on and on,
we see much buzz or anyone,
but mustn't laugh and mustn't cry;
a diva's heart can break and die.

Her vanity takes her along,
that narcissistic, she's not wrong,
and when her ghost has blown her head,
no tail in tow will trail her tread.

Outer inspirations

What becomes of memories

No question where we're going to,
the prophecies know when and who,
however memories may appear
until we are no longer here.

Will memories alone remain
as pictures or as true as plain,
will happenings be kept by them
or stay themselves alone ad rem?

So many retrospections see
one thing discretionarily,
and this will not unite all those,
since those can't share what one keeps close.

What ever was will stay as past,
as well as all its pictures last,
it happens once and gets recalled
in line with all that is installed.

Outer inspirations

Falling masks

Masks are falling through the night,
darkness brings them into light,
laughing, crying is their gaze,
overcome my silent place.

Gloomily attracting me,
more than day's reality,
my surrounding forces dreams
so that fright chokes off my screams.

Being taken by this spell
senses find no mood to dwell;
listening to the whispering gloom
they don't now by what or whom.

They are dancing around like mad,
spreading fear I've never had,
I sweat blood and I feel cold
as I guess what they unfold.

Then the quiet's back again,
all is gone that seemed insane,
but no silence in my heart;
deep inside I've grown apart.

Outer inspirations

Nothing happens anymore

Nothing happens over there.
But there's light behind the panes.
Yet, no shadows, light could share.
Shadows are of hope that faints.

Look, one window's getting black.
That's a temporary phase.
Will the one who left come back?
He's not gone, but out of place.

Many now have left the scene.
Someone else will save the light.
Does he know what it might mean?
Do not think about his right.

Seemingly now all have gone,
Well, shut up you bovine fool.
Darkness won't conceal what's on.
Now, who cares what busts their pool?

Outer inspirations

Sold fate

You are not much cop hereby,
we look through you without trace,
have a drink and don't ask why,
then we see what's taken place.

Next you need a destiny,
there are many fates to start.
What can suit your tragedy?
Being a lost son makes smart.

An affliction makes all feel,
fractures of your legs are trite,
must be something hard to heal:
heartless you can gain odd light.

Let us drive your spirit mad,
most important for the show,
otherwise you'll lose the thread,
money your remains love, though.

Faux pas

Faux Pas!
Oh boy ...
... The truth is afterwards no joy.
Élat?
Just know!
It's actually no blame to show.

Don't mind!
Was weak.
My honesty must have a leak.
Unwind!
And hey,
All take it easy all the way.

Gone without an end

We're always looking for an end,
which gets topped off and keeps its form;
if point of start or just a bend,
what we expect is but a norm.

A reason is what all ends need
and consequence is needed too;
as long as time joins steps and feet,
we may accept what's coming true.

However, sometimes urges fill
what we expect with pointless facts;
that leaves us to the bitter pill
that sometimes nothing else reacts.

Outer inspirations

Without commitment

Through a funnel the condition screws
own disposition in the twist
of internalisation
down to the
fall
of
pre-
oc-
cu-
pied
Ideas
to end in
brief overestimation
far away and without commitment in respect of times in time.

Outer inspirations

Whiningly cold-blooded

A blood stream drags at its decay,
one cannot watch and goes astray;
out of the corner of his eye
his view flees cruelty to spy.

He hopes for more, his deed he apes,
wants to escape but still he gapes,
in his asylum he feels home,
remembers pictures he can roam.

He hangs about from street to street,
madly disgusted by his deed,
such keeling over dead makes sick,
why is that dying beastly big.

His home he reaches tired out,
seems satisfied but hardly proud,
he opens windows, cuts the light,
but ghosts don't fade into the night.

In darkness they beat up his heart,
he dreams of pain, while breathing hard,
when waking up, he's dead again,
he cleans his knife - has breakfast then.

Outer inspirations

Black holes in our head

Billionfold the world encloses
eyesight, loving or in hate;
watching time that space composes,
paired they know each other's fate.

Light comes in and darkness keeps it,
fading somewhere to remain;
where it stays remains as secret
at that foreign place, the brain.

Shifty-eyed they roll and wander
all throughout a vivid view,
weight themselves as self-responder,
rein in any little clue.

Vulnerable but intensive,
bright or silent, proud or dead,
tears at sights that seem ostensive:
It's the black holes in our head.

Outer inspirations

Distorting world

Globally our world's distorting,
structures break into our times,
and ingeniously retorting
we take rhythms just for rhymes.

Are things going on when moving?
We gain knowledge just to keep.
Link by link, we climb improving
how to fall from grace - and deep.

We get shaped by senses' flooding,
pressing breath through tangled mass;
there where efforts may be thudding,
sense gets lost in lusty buzz.

Held in check we fight in struggle,
we're confused as things remain,
think that nothing makes us juggle,
crisscross we live on in vain.

Outer inspirations

What's the stake

Listen, what's to talk about,
let's debate for issue's sake,
utter stuff that makes it proud,
impartiality's the stake.

Then the centre spins around,
won't find truth in you and me,
gathering what we have found,
it takes clues to verity.

Untouched facts and figures grow,
knowledge, slowly aiming high,
someone dives into its flow,
shouting in an instant 'I!"

There the heavy spot is set,
and the others can't escape,
stumble soon into this tread,
and in vaunt they lose their shape.

Overgrowing is their fuss,
writhing in its own concern,
individuals discuss
while the wannabes just yearn.

That what it was all about
now makes way for chatty swizz,
and where hearts made knowledge proud,
wisenheimers show their bliss.

Outer inspirations

Off the stage

The stage is empty seats are cold,
the actress looks for inner peace,
her Julia's heart was long since old,
and paid by huge applause's ease.

The curtain logged the living act,
a headless role cannot survive;
beyond, she's figure to a fact,
on stage her love was all her life.

Her Romeo passed too soon each night,
she followed wishing not to wake,
a death, much sweeter than day's fight,
which bitterly she can't forsake.

And now the final heaven fell,
frenetic screams in whirling shine,
one smile gets human in this hell:
The prompter asks her to some wine.

Outer inspirations

View resistance

Somewhere in the distance
we expect so much to see;
views are just resistance,
hiding space where we can't be.

Close your eyes, remember
that it all is but a view;
far beyond dead ember
lies much more without ado.

On screen hubbub

There is hubbub on the screen,
powers up the micro scene;
as a sigh gets sense to win,
little fortune makes souls thin.

Life then blows remains away,
wasted nonsense goes astray,
bodies go asleep as flesh,
waking up in dreamless trash.

Outer inspirations

Out of 404

Here's nothing more,
in four-o-four.
Just you and I?
Let's see and try.

A trick by chance,
no spurious glance,
and soon aligned,
each others' mind.

No web to roam,
we are at home.
Where are you, though,
how can I know?

Go through the door,
to find what for,
then move ahead,
I'll find your tread.

Outer inspirations

Conquered

Finally they have betrayed
visions made to renegade,
not to fight for freedom's chance,
but for their oppressors' lance.

Toadying, they longed for gold
as their country's wounds got sold;
rotters, wasting rotten fates,
changed tradition into aids.

Modern wise men lead the board
between poverty and sword,
in their pockets, system's prey,
gaiters decorate their way.

Ask one where his sorrow lives,
he knows what tomorrow briefs,
and his history's destiny
is no longer his to see.

Outer inspirations

Scrutinized future

Have you ever realized
what the screams are begging for,
is your future scrutinized
by the chances we adore?

Back then, also you were there,
in those times of innocence,
as it happened in despair:
thinking freedom fence by fence.

Don't you really want to see
whether deeds can conquer words,
not by talk of melody,
but by songs that nothing hurts.

Won't it matter to your hearts
why your history's never learnt?
Ask us once to cut your cards,
and then deal what we have spurned.

Outer inspirations

Politically messed up

They still believe in it today,
in that what they had wished in dreams,
and jovially eat up their prey
of new-rich values' lost esteems.

Not missing anything, well paid,
they actually do not know by whom,
politically messed up and played
in ease of their cerebral boom.

The real spirit, long since lost,
can't challenge obsolete ideas,
the future's done on past times' cost,
and problems' smoothing no one fears.

Good faith complacently may sigh
in idle talk with loosened buzz;
this is not even reason why
the world discusses modern fuss.

Outer inspirations

In rumour's place

A beam gets warped around a point,
which somewhat somewhere dipped in space;
no light-years' and no darkness' joint
sets wise ideas in rumours' place.

Distorted figures can't equate
the calculation without dream;
good formulas need to be paid
to keep the world facts how they seem.

Who wants to understand a thing
when watching it is good enough?
It's there and does not have to cling
to minds in petty-minded stuff.

Ghosts and spirits

In between old walls and paper,
hoping spirits in dried glue,
at a window sits an aper,
dreaming of a magic clue.

He is watching what he wishes,
ghosts replace the outside life,
crackling sounds make him capricious,
spirits live but ghosts survive.

Outer inspirations

Merchandized pain

A rest of pain gets merchandised,
infirmity can hardly speak,
some vapid jokes are oversized,
the show is great - the shown one weak.

The audience has learnt to hope,
its consternation throws applause;
it hits what poor man's truth can't cope,
the limelight that his shadows cause.

The seats are empty, time gone by,
and poured out laughter, washed away;
the studio sends every sigh
to homes where wheel- and armchairs stay.

Spoiled words

There were these words I promptly lost,
now I can't find them to my cost,
I wish to clean up their remains,
exchanging truth in foreign brains.

Adjusted worlds are always round,
no past of presence to be found,
the atmosphere gets filthy though,
just breathing it won't stop the show.

I ask, what happened, finally;
I look inside myself and see
a truly noncommittal fraud
as patch-work-talk has come to naught.

Stalker

My room's still listening to me,
the window cannot calm my view,
and infiltrating noises see
hysteria in fear of you.

Through dusky gleams a shadow crawls,
just trees or yet an insane take,
you meanly grin from patterned walls
since you know every step I make.

A torchlight's ray bursts every crack,
if fancied or by real threat,
it hits me in my nervous wreck
while snooping in my tortured head.

It waits in all surrounding things,
your spirit they cannot deny,
in corners' darkness notion swings,
it sucks my haggard conscience dry.

I crouch and almost fall apart,
my lungs don't dare to take a breath:
Why must this cold hand grab my heart
and choke my fright almost to death?

Outer inspirations

Last writing people

The very last writing people
will draw their stories
with their fingers
in the sand of earth's remains;
they won't know too much anymore,
they won't ask too much anymore,
so that the wind light-heartedly
will take the signs along
into their truth ...

Gliese 581g

Living space in brains,
separating
desert day
from freezing night:
Nothing that remains
by debating;
blown away
by light-years' might.

Wolf in sheep's clothing

There's a spirit in his eyes,
dressed in fluffy, feigned disguise.
Welcome! shouts the stupid heap,
who are you - we are the sheep.

As he keeps his profile low,
an ignored one in a row,
he may play a faithful mate,
and his scent seems sheep-like, straight.

Unexpectedly, a jolt,
instincts force him to unfold;
and the pelt turns inside out,
but the bleating gets just loud.

Brain death genius

And the genius gets constrained
by ideas of theories,
mental agony is chained,
drives resentment to its knees.

They are lost as time goes by,
never felt salvation's boon,
and the world spins without 'why'
in its vacuum-cocoon.

In this sphere of liberty,
which no thinker needs to fear,
brains may die, but souls stay free
since their spirits find a tear.

Outer inspirations

Media hyped catastrophes

These media-hyped catastrophes
are TV-ratings' number one,
and calmed by news presenter's ease
in case the tragedy's soon gone.

However once there'll be a surge
that maybe's just a harbinger,
but then the news will no more purge
the truth - and fled, the news bringer.

Another factory day

It was just another day,
closing finally the gate,
and a last one without say
drags his feet home to his fate.

Just a factory's light keeps guard,
clocking minutes that don't count,
fades in gloom of morning's start,
shadows feel no light around.

Rut by rut converges then,
what the evening won't regret;
that the stamp clock lacks one man,
will the break time snack forget.

Outer inspirations

The runner

The signal! And his legs eject,
he watches out for left and right,
he brings his heart into effect,
then it gets quiet on each side.

The images speed past his face
while breath in headwind causes ache,
and gravity makes way for space
when energy could almost break.

Imbued by muscles' power pack,
the will to win then gets compressed,
each tread extends from calf to neck,
integrity is victory's nest.

There's no look back, no barrier,
the tunnel-view ahead is all,
the aim defines its area,
the final point it soon will call.

No disbelief can stop the run,
and self-trust thrusts it to the front,
it works as body-bullet's gun,
'cause faster is what needs to want.

And finally the scene gets wide,
before the finish, it exults,
and then it spins around in light,
confirms reward of winner's pulse.

Outer inspirations

The shrink

The literate pundit tears his hair,
well bleached by modern theories,
for cash, he plods through pure despair,
with knowledge money can't increase.

He tries to understand the moods
when shaping mental ignorance,
and conversation digs for roots,
it pokes about in nescience.

He empathizes to allure
what session's stretching bank expands,
disorders may evade the cure,
'cause somewhere else they find some sense.

New courage gets desensitized
to find what was long overdue,
neuroses can be supervised
by tests projecting healer's view.

His face can flatter all his skill,
'How does it feel for you', it smirks:
If still insane, if foozled will,
who knows to feel a strangers quirks?

Inner beast

Please imagine, now and here,
there's a stranger's voice in you,
soon disgorging what you were,
and your skin gets scaly too.

Pressure's pulsing through your eyes,
hearts are boiling in your chest,
limbs are bursting through their size,
claws rip screams out of your rest.

What will live and what is prey,
what is actor, what is role?
Dragging off your slow decay,
parts won't die within your soul.

Powerful and almost crooked,
throbbing in your agony,
there's a torso that has spooked
deep inside, now breaking free.

Secretly the creature scrams,
leaving germs around the spot,
'till the time, which future jams,
shows a new infected slot.

Outer inspirations

Burping joy

Look, the trashy window lights,
flashing ghosts touch up the truth,
mulled wine, calming down the fights,
burping joy and brawling youth.

Look, that funfair wannabe,
in disguise of Christmas cant;
dragging off a plastic tree
may distract from thoughts that rant.

Look, those faces, made to serve
while a cheeky brat shows off:
Wanna have!, it has the nerve,
gets its gift as big rip-off.

Look, ways home, a holy string,
victory of feasting trance,
someone lost a silly thing,
feeds a waif in crouched stance.

Spoiled time

Why are you in search of ways
scrunching nature all the time?
Stand by mirrors of your place,
in essentials of your clime.

All around you find dense wood,
which you anyway won't roam;
far beyond new fields with food,
as you moan your words blow foam.

Miracles, is all you want,
and your logic doesn't care;
you believe the world gets fond
as you hush up its despair.

Wannabes is what you are,
varnished curiosity;
truly faith is what you bar
during times' velocity.

Outer inspirations

End time Advent

It burns ... it burns,
it's burning everywhere,
the waiting is severe,
because nobody yearns.

It smokes ... it smokes,
the world is smoking on,
no Lord in sight who's won,
to trash what light evokes.

So cold ... so cold,
the stubs are cold and dead,
reunion's day makes sad,
not paid what Advent's sold.

Advent ... Advent
it's done before it flees,
it rocks calamities,
until the mood is spent.

My starlight's rising

I see a starlight rising
beyond my aimless mood,
but waiting hope's resizing
the ones that know to hoot.

I see horizons burning,
a fire of good luck;
while artfulness keeps yearning,
fools hate when they don't chuck.

I see the ashes glowing
until their last remain;
some sparks will still be showing
how they light up their pain.

What we should fear

Was it here, was it there?
I don't know, I do not care.
Was it now, was it then?
Seems to be out of the plan.

Was it true, was it wrong?
Say, to what did it belong?
Was it new, was it old?
Anyway not warm or cold.

Was it just, or a 'must',
who's the one in whom we trust?
He's not there, he's not here,
that is what we all should fear.

Outer inspirations

The golden age

The golden age above the years,
projecting into clouds of tears,
has taken every root along,
no matter what is right or wrong.

When pouring out, the heavens cry,
but metal's hard while moods are shy;
they're growing somewhere in between,
the rain is just a rainbow's spleen.

The times of levelling down are odd,
and yet they make the masses nod,
define a colour to succeed,
contrastless views won't touch the greed.

It seems as if this world could stay,
the shadows feed heroic prey,
but when the light goes down again,
the biggest contrast finds its drain.

Narcissism

In confidence the mirror stands
by kisses lips cannot evade;
the heart is racing in its trance
and rapt by egocentric raid.

If lost in lust, if lost in pain,
it flinches from each foreign view;
the self-image is loud and vain,
the soul gets smashed when eyes burn through.

A light that someone else may touch
is always worth it to collect;
a cautious hint 'don't take too much'
might hurt the smugly intellect.

And even altruistic streaks
cannot belie the tricky soul;
the weakness such a helper seeks
gets utilized for helper's goal.

True happiness is no more choice,
but waste of time can't realize;
and frenzy of a selfish voice
makes greedy thoughts monopolize.

Yet lonely stays an empty shell,
not capable to share its world;
a cave for a psychotic will
where lifeless beauty gets unfurled.

Outer inspirations

Just a cloud

It's just a cloud, don't worry, dear,
the worriers are still far away,
too far to recognize or fear,
it's just a cloud, which shades a day.

The sky's still there, look in between,
don't hope, just say that it's all right,
don't think what anybody's seen,
the plumes have simply missed the light.

Oh' please don't cry, it will not hurt,
you're wasting your disturbing mind,
allergic thoughts make you alert,
their fallout makes your vision blind.

My dear, walk on, your way is fine,
the storm abates, and I'm grown old;
don't blame the things that keep in line
for what I've taught, which someone told.

Outer inspirations

Heap of meat

Vanity dehumanizes,
claiming social finishing,
while the creature sympathises
with its need, a living thing.

Struggling manners on a fine line
have two sides to topple down,
one uncovers fat as life's sign,
one puts head cheese in a gown.

In between there must be culture
socialising on its way;
narrow-minded gets a sculpture
when embarrassed by child's play.

To transgress can mean to stumble
flesh gets crooked, smiles get wry,
I like flesh when spirits humble,
shaping faces with a lie.

Outer inspirations

Village funfair

Yet a drop of rousing crowd,
puke and litter in the street,
basses scatter every shout,
at the beer stall brawlers meet.

Steely carrousels debunked,
peeing drunkards miss their cup,
panties behind wagons, junked,
crying fit when cashing up.

Someone trashes someone's child,
cannot call a spade a spade,
nerves stab feelings, going wild,
busybodies mediate.

Gradually the streetlights win,
fighting every neon ramp,
rancid sweetness in between,
sweepers shoo away a tramp.

Grand finale sounds insane,
sends remaining heroes home,
catchy songs fade lane by lane,
blue lights calm a lonesome mome.

Outer inspirations

Pirates

The waves reflect the pallid gleam,
and moonlight watches nightly souls;
the seamen, following the beam,
some others follow darker goals.

They float along in trappy peace,
their senses, lost in home bound thoughts;
just water strengthens vastness' ease,
and fear is for those shapeless lords.

A careful smile hopes for the best,
the captain and his first mate stay;
their sailors have deserved a rest
while everything will be ok.

Yet deep below a moment waits,
some evil eyes, which no one knows;
the fight, too short to warn the mates,
good hope at home but vainly grows.

Beyond the skyline they move on,
a keel shares streams of deathly quiet;
the seagulls cry, the ocean's won,
the curse has swallowed woe and light.

Outer inspirations

Secrets

The secret that a surface keeps
lets us imagine anything;
it's non existent as it heaps
alternatives to everything.

The more we watch the more we see,
if we don't ask, it has no spell;
a secret truly cannot be
if we look <u>through</u>, not <u>at</u> its shell.

A riddle needs a logic way,
which finally breaks through in threads,
however secrets want to play
with fantasy that stays in heads.

Therefore a secret can't be solved,
and even if, we fancy more;
the spirit is too much involved
in claims that riddles may ignore.

Outer inspirations

Balance of inhumanity

Winkle pickers give the beat,
cut in money's potency,
walk a tightrope for the greed,
balance inhumanity.

Too young spirits poshly feast,
immaturely flying high,
shakeouts leave all trust diseased,
clever smirks make faces wry.

Speed befalls the right of time
as efficiency kills tries,
prigs go on about their prime
'till their age they must revise.

Late experience regrets
nothing but mistaken trends;
humans on which no one bets,
vanish from commercial sense.

Soon run down the end is shut,
keeping what has driven it;
liquidated, to be cut,
yet a rope that fell to quit.

Outer inspirations

Where the wind blows

Where'll take us a sudden gust
when it leaves us speechless then;
is there sense below the blast
that stands truth beyond our ken?

When I let it blow me away,
I am clever as before;
if, despite the blow, I stay,
truthfulness might preen and bore.

Well, I don't deliberate
brazen breezes on the scout,
but I'm getting weak too late
as serenity finds out.

Pages in an empty book

They swore the big fidelity,
around the altar, gaudy trash,
with cake that fed reality,
gave birth too early to their flesh.

They still demand romantic life,
but look like yeast bread, baked too long
while playing love from strife to strife:
Two in a boat are hardly wrong.

They finally just need to live
to drink their dose, by hook or crook;
and cling to somewhat they can't give,
like pages in a wordless book.

Outer inspirations

Majestic sledge

For beauty they pay every price,
in confidence to devil's pledge;
a simple being, otherwise,
gets carved by a majestic sledge.

He uses flesh and skin and bone,
to cover heartache's ruthless will;
the heart itself feels much too 'lone
to spurn cosmetic's overkill.

Discreetly working, day by day,
the evil signs each winning smile;
the well scarred faces in decay
are anything but juvenile.

No fate can stay incognito
when life discovers its hideout;
while vicious traits of wrinkles grow,
the demon seeds another sprout.

He does not care about the few
who finally might shed some tears;
he only made a dream come true
to demonize the truth with fears.

Outer inspirations

Washed out towels

Washed out flowers on old towels,
decorating kitchen blues,
backyard balconies throw vowels,
cigarettes blow time in dues.

Television cries for stupor,
it controls remote controls,
makes the switcher find it super,
standing by his prepaid roles.

Smoke has greyed the curtained border,
like the city suburbs' past,
in between the world's in order,
well, as long as towels last.

Time frames

If everything depends on time,
it self destroys its endless chime;
and yet its end cannot persist,
another start it would have missed.

What comes will go, endurance counts,
but in the end still silence sounds;
there'll be no real eternity,
there's but all worlds of times to be.

Outer inspirations

Longing's sore

Movies no one watches anymore,
stacking unfulfilling memories,
roles that squirm with pain of longing's sore
feel like disempowered wannabes.

On and on the mighty fever burnt,
every 'Wow!' subsided much too fast,
fascinating highs, which lows returned,
in between the source of lifeless past.

Windows out of life into the day
carry all its shine in dungeons night;
rushing streets engulf what heartbeats pray,
dragging shadows off that had some light.

Calculation forms commerce and need,
hardly touched by true integrity;
compromised realisations feed,
also giving parts of dreams esprit.

Thus the wasted talents struggle on,
honestly believing in their claim,
wrongfully forgotten when they're gone,
we just see their ghosts in limelight's fame.

Outer inspirations

Nobody

Nobody is on the street,
be aware he's on the go,
everybody shares one speed,
Nobody may be too slow.

Nobody has lost his mind,
seems like he's out of control,
everybody knows to find,
Nobody may seek a goal.

Nobody is evident,
look at him, he's not dressed up,
everybody shapes the trend,
Nobody may leave the hub.

Nobody is made of flesh,
moves his ugly body parts,
everybody shuns each clash,
Nobody may mind his heart.

Outer inspirations

Characters alive

Leave the acting to the act
and the actors all alone;
that makes storylines affect
what the actors call their own.

Leave them truly words to find
out of free reality,
leave them fiction to unwind
that is only theirs to see.

Waste or value

Another day has found its dusk,
a place where time can stay and ask,
an intermediate farewell
that cleans the outside of a shell.

And while the hubbubs disappear,
the moves inside are getting clear;
not any longer torn and jarred,
the light ahead becomes a guard.

The shadows float into the sheen,
are spurred and powered from within.
Who knows what will be waiting soon?
Just waste or value to cocoon.

Outer inspirations

Sunday walk

Silence,
step by step,
laughter glittering through words,
breezes,
silencing,
freeing freedom from remorse.

Whisper,
step by step,
volumes speaking cosy flirts,
silence,
wandering,
sentences that do not force.

Silence,
step by step,
overtaken by odd birds,
air draught,
worrying,
loudly preaching next day's course.

Contradiction's destiny

Beauty keeps and covers life,
evanescence haunts its way;
those who're fighting to survive
will be hunters – will be prey.

Contradiction's destiny
seems as cruel as lost hope;
from this point of view we see
just the treasure, not its scope.

Between rising and decline
there's one peak we all adore,
it's a bloom, a smile or shine,
a minority of more.

Only far beyond our scenes
we could find, apart from Gods,
that we live a mean of means,
leopards can't change their spots.

What you feel is what you get,
even losses just count time;
being happy, being sad
share one tone in all the chime.

Outer inspirations

Room four hundred four

Not found
in room four hundred four,
not found,
all friendship must have gone,
too bound,
gets ripped in parts that bore,
too bound
means loneliness has won.

No sign
beyond the glaring screen,
no sign
of authenticity,
each line
of digits faked a scene,
each line
led into crookery.

Our truth
goes on in real time,
our truth
is nothing lies could share,
to soothe
our vanity is prime,
to soothe
it shields from shallow care.

Cold turkey

The twitching frozen eyes
can almost not resist;
the force that covers lies
makes quivering lips insist.

The longing must convulse,
- a shuttered embryo -;
from conscience suffering pulse
keeps heartbeats on the go.

Insanity gets ripped
as pain is feeling truth;
both sides are well equipped,
but none of them is smooth.

No point of free return,
the soul is banned from pain,
it just goes on to burn
in every tainted vein.

It's neither death nor life
what suddenly brings peace;
a void has left the strife,
its blessing cannot please.

The vice then leaves the head
its wrinkles, parched and old;
the body may be glad,
humanity stays cold.

Outer inspirations

Bewitched

Bewitched, a way might search for more
than its direction makes believe;
all over skewed from top to floor,
imagination may conceive.

The magic twists around the pull,
which, sober, only finds an end;
but well entwined to overrule,
its hole saves fantasy's content.

Educing shivers from a dwell
unfolds a strange and hidden weal,
its comfortably haunting spell
may open a forsaken seal.

When finally the exit nears,
it closes all that lies behind;
what went ahead has left our fears
and enters memories to unwind.

Outer inspirations

Blind followers

Someone screams and lifts his thumb,
others follow due to yearning;
I can't sense them and feel numb:
What's the point that is concerning?

As they shout I look for help,
need to follow some reflection,
but to delve into their yelp
can just mean to lose my action.

Anyway, I'm lame at all
yet before I must surrender;
just my thoughts survive my fall,
my ideas kill their defender.

There's a way out of the field
that the mass-control won't capture
since the milestones it might yield
are too factual for rapture.

I pick all they can't delete,
and escape this supervision;
no one follows my retreat
since they think there's no decision.

Outer inspirations

Stretched smile

Underneath a well stretched smile,
underneath its coloured line,
lids aren't able to beguile
since the face is just design.

In disguise, a wilting shell,
cannot feed the choking core,
petrifies the scandal's spell,
spends no longing anymore.

All that happened long ago
has been freezing through the years,
but still outcast pupils grow,
or they shrink in search of tears.

When we look into such eyes,
putting facts and face aside;
they won't tell us any lies,
if there's darkness, if there's light.

Outer inspirations

Lobbyism

Threads from underneath dark roofs,
dangling deep in all the world,
search for democratic spoofs,
puppets' slips of tongues get burled.

Seizing opportunity,
they are ghosts between the facts,
dance in lofty company,
on the strings that move the acts.

They debate and they make plans,
with good will that can't deny
that they'll overcome all sense;
wooden heads don't blink an eye.

When their final curtain falls,
no one's there to wave goodbye;
and the strings release the dolls,
new elected ones may try.

Briefly these will show regret
for bad forces in their mould;
soon they're captured thread by thread,
telling what they're getting told.

Outer inspirations

Famous clues

When is a clue a famous word
as aphoristic artefact,
although it's easy and not blurred
and could suit birdbrain's intellect?

It is no power of insight
that binds together easiness,
and not a pseudo-change by light,
which lyrically calms each distress.

Expression quickly fades away,
in an aha-reaction's Wow!
Astonishment is gone astray
before it finds the clue's know-how.

Again it sounds across our minds,
again it has just little claim;
nobody thinks behind the blinds
about its trivial logic-frame.

The spirit of such famous clue
is finally what rocks the crowd;
a fabled name comes right on cue,
no matter what it speaks out loud.

Outer inspirations

Poverty itself

When poverty itself gets poor,
it's lost because it is secure;
around our houses winds shoo doubts,
cloak streets in secrecy of shrouds;
sad poverty gets cold and poor,
a childlike heart beats warm and shouts.

The roar becomes a mighty storm
we're safe, and sated we conform;
behind the merlons of our tower,
we call the poor and don't get sour;
but poverty is just a worm,
the child's too close and without power.

Then far away we find our bliss,
which takes us back to what we miss;
the path of virtue brings us fun
when our due is on the run;
a farce of poverty it is,
the child gets pale when hope is done.

Real poverty lends wings to naught,
no wind, no storm keeps light we bought;
it stops at nothing we achieve
when living off what we should give;
at last poor poverty is fought
when dead eyes close a child's belief.

Outer inspirations

Bound and pained

Time that tightly gets enchained
rounds the vastness night and day;
vehemently bound and pained,
our world is urged to sway.

Deep below, a throbbing heart,
pounding into ways to go,
almost prising life apart,
struggling over debts to show.

Round and round it gets ballooned,
light expands across the sphere,
blames world's pull for being ruined,
blurring all the atmosphere.

Wasted power, yawing loud,
weakened by its bluish fat,
popping after bursting out
of its oversize it had.

Outer inspirations

State of the art

Now, finally mankind has conquered the peaks,
and sharply divided the world breaks apart;
what money once bleached is now showing first leaks,
becoming obsessed by its state of the art.

Big values are falling and crushing in vain
while ruins can't find any time to lean on;
these should have been virtues but suffer from pain,
and leaving the ashes cold they are just gone.

However, all time's perpendicular rules,
with power it puts life's ideas in its place;
there's law and there's order but nature beats fools,
and finally history is king on time's ways.

The wandering anger leaves spirits too sad,
their exodus helplessly finds no way out;
when withering grain poisons underdone bread,
it feeds only bodies, no souls to be proud.

The freedom to compromise is getting pale
while compromised weakness gets used to set traps;
the atmosphere's thuggish, but all must inhale,
aggression falls into their virtuous laps.

What's peace and what's war is a question of naught,
and death will no longer tell evil from good;
it vilifies triumphs and worships no lord,
it's that what we make it: the mastermind's food.

Outer inspirations

Shine on for the child

Shine on for the child, shine on,
far away and still so small;
where your future's hope stands tall,
shine on, shine when all has gone.

When the days are getting grey,
all a child needs is calm light;
just glow warmly through the night,
makes the li'l one laugh and pray.

Then stay tranquil in your star,
sing a rhyme to light the scene;
children love it to chime in
when the tune is not bizarre.

Shine on for the child, shine on,
grown up still before assumed,
either shining or yet doomed,
never leave its light be gone.

The wannabe writer

Watch him, sitting, writing there,
what a splendid specimen,
watch this artist in his sphere,
as much unknown as he can.

Like a fancy beauty spot
upon pale complexioned skin,
as a world's proleptic lot,
his profoundness he burns in.

All he does seems secret though,
zoned by his phenomenon;
those who're hoodwinked by his show
find him as a random one.

Even so, he gets his kick
from beyond creativeness;
keeping odd thoughts in his neck,
peeps at gazer's nosiness.

When he's begged enough for heed,
he may quit the silly game:
Not much white that ink could feed,
but a pen to prove poor fame.

Outer inspirations

Heart's blood

Dip your heart, to gain much more,
in this lake of longing blood,
find out new ideas' galore,
make pain your creative flood.

On and on, these heartbeats go,
throughout tides of living art,
give it time enough to grow,
let it live off every part.

Then experience your work,
it is timeless, deep inside;
do not chat since that could burke
stimuli, which need their quiet.

Now lift up from blood to tears
what the act has made of it,
natural and free of fears,
just be touched by what you did.

Inner inspirations

Inner inspirations

Guardian of affliction, 133
Final certitude, 133
Latitudinarian, 134
With whom, 135
Too much sense, 136
We won't know, 137
Act of laughter, 137
My heart, 138
Vanished treasures, 139
Letting go, 139
Shadows of memories, 140
Onetime sign, 141
Below the butterfly, 142
My window and me, 143
One way, 144
Horizons, 145
Swoosh of thoughts, 146
Freedom below skies, 147
Path into consciousness, 148
Japanese blossoms falling, 149
Sates of mind, 150
Short hand's tip, 150
Dream on, my free ideas, 151
Morning peace, 152
Facing, 153
Is it here?, 154
Heart surgeon, 155
Smallest light, 156
Not just a simple smile, 157
True wishes, 158
Pounding will, 159
The scribbler, 160
Beyond the day, 161
City fright, 162
Remind my heart, 163
Along the clouds, 163
Lifetime bloom, 164
My inner self, 164
Out of my house, 165
Beside you, 166
Under bridges, 166
Get lost with me, 167
Bluish night, 167
Windows at the wall, 168
Repatriation, 169
In memories, 170
Home bound, 171
An undiscovered land, 172
I-Instance, 173
Way to salvation, 174
A tiny dream, 174
Hand in hand, 175
After all I am, 176
My final love, 177
Three ways, 178
Different home land, 178
Scent of time, 179
Another poem for my heart, 180

Inner inspirations

Guardian of affliction

I'm the guardian of affliction,
under moon shine your free world,
and its dark becomes addiction
where feigned pictures get unfurled.

I am new silk round old leather,
even if that stood the test,
I'm the climate of your weather,
what is worst and what is best?!

I am waspish when detected,
and in patronizing mood,
I love colours, wound-infected,
'cause my madness is a hoot.

Final certitude

Horizons, overgrown,
silence finds deserted peace;
a circle on its own
shares a glass of wine to ease.

Spirits feed the core,
wisdom loses knowledge's pride;
certitude is more:
wishes those a last good night.

Inner inspirations

Latitudinarian

They find him interesting, indeed,
they find him out of social range;
but he supports what they don't need:
a review - while the others change.

He is appreciated yet
as long his words are mental smoke;
'cause there is nothing to regret
since offered friendship is a joke.

A modern world needs modern peace,
and modern thoughts are well prepared;
a freak can absolutely please,
it's sometimes hip to be dead scared.

However, when the time has come
to suit the action to the word,
the melody denies the hum;
was nice to hear but never heard.

The glasses leave a final cheer,
their smile is looking for some crutch,
the eyebrows perk to hide the fear:
was nice with him but yet too much.

Inner inspirations

With whom

With whom may I share deep ideas?
Are written by my secret heart;
but they feel limited by fears
that lonely thoughts could break apart.

In every sentence I create
another heartbeat shows a sign,
and confidence in what I've made
contains a part that is not mine.

From verse to verse I dream around
and feel this visitor inside;
I spend us time in what we've found,
predicted from a distant might.

Perhaps I wake up in my mind
tomorrow on a brand new day,
and still whatever I may find
is guided by an overlay.

Inner inspirations

Too much sense

Can't stay off and can't go on,
something keeps me in suspense,
each idea is all in one,
far too little, too much sense.

Freely stumbling, counting days,
found so many crossing points;
multiplied and aimless ways
are fulfilments of the joints.

Blown up thoughts plug empty clues,
get me out of my ideas,
I'm a snail in running shoes,
marking time where speed just smears.

Everything is spread around,
I may pick up this and that,
proud to gather what I've found,
useless to complete a thread.

Time is passing, so I am,
looking for a thing to blame,
take my rhinestone as my gem,
secrets may fulfil my aim.

Inner inspirations

We won't know

We never will be knowing
how human's conscience once began,
as well as we'll be going;
the final child in every man.

We're asking for tomorrow
and leave our memories behind;
the last one, full of sorrow,
will not be seen since he is blind.

When earthmen found their dead end,
a giant, red, will swallow all.
Who'll count the stars beforehand
until his breathlessness must crawl?

Act of laughter

On chuckling lips, some swaying joy,
not yet disclosed, a little coy;
in face's movement, some delay,
is curious about the play.

A smile may tug at curtain's seam,
behind it, an exciting gleam;
beholders now can almost find
what in a moment will unwind.

And then a laughter rocks the stage,
releases stars out of their cage,
the soul can finally run free,
the limelight shows heart's comedy.

Inner inspirations

My heart

My heart,
it beats like mad
and flails around,
relying on its blood.
My heart,
in stumbling tread,
has lost its sound
in veins, a soothing flood.

My heart,
it tamely beats
and drifts away
within a major flush.
My heart
it lamely cheats;
a tainted prey
with rhythm slowed by hush.

My heart
is still unfed,
but almost drowned
in misanthropic mud.
My heart,
again upset,
indeed unbound
to find again its rut.

Vanished treasures

Those treasures of days that have vanished
aren't questioning since they've been banished,
but some are still guiding my present
as secrets, which sometimes are pleasant.

They're waiting as guards in a distance,
but never as lifetime's resistance;
secured in my thoughts of desire,
my bastions of calm I admire.

In unobserved moments I ponder
if anything else could be fonder;
these treasures then strengthen what matters,
which otherwise too often shatters.

Letting go

Running, simply running,
the path alone knows best;
feeling, simply feeling
my thoughts, which have no crest.

Resting, simply resting
in hope within my speed;
knowing, simply knowing
there is no need to beat.

Being, simply being
as I've been living on;
smiling, simply smiling,
already almost gone.

Inner inspirations

Shadows of memories

In shadows of our memories
we feel secure or lost;
all life ahead, of fear or ease,
depends on lifeline's cost.

In shadows of intimacy
we dare to know what's on;
are hard on our hypocrisy
until our truth is gone.

In shadows of our simple minds
we may divine what's right.
But isn't it just closing blinds
to get us out of sight?

In shadows of the universe
there's buried what we search;
we tempt our darkness, that's our curse,
to find what we can't merge.

Inner inspirations

Onetime sign

A wink, a pair of eyes,
a shadow on the fly,
a face, which otherwise
not even caused a sigh.

Was working on my mind,
I thought it was a quirk,
but quirks can just make blind,
my sense I could not burke.

The years have passed my face,
and memories decline,
yet somewhere in time's haze
I keep that onetime sign.

One hope with highs and lows,
depending on my mood,
in each my sureness grows,
I share somebody's root.

The darkness is just black
but deeper into nights;
this pair of eyes calls back
my single-sided sights.

Inner inspirations

Below the butterfly

Below the butterfly
we both forgot the world
in leaves that built our sky;
the light hung so unfurled.

Embedded, soft and deep,
surrounded just by blooms,
true love prepared our sleep,
it whispered through perfumes.

The wind took shivers' lust,
cooled down its temperament,
we hummed a song at last,
and soon were somnolent.

Not woken up, like numb,
I still know how to yearn;
the world but made me jump
as it began to turn.

Inner inspirations

My window and me

I'm standing by my window,
we're surrounded by the dusk,
my mind within the frame-show,
pushed through days from task to task.

In rooms behind my being
all my time has left remains,
in every little something
I can find what holds the reins.

Odd wishes pass and vanish,
dusk adjusts their highs and lows,
some duties I might banish,
all we want the evening shows.

The three of us, together:
the spirit in the frame and I;
I show my mind the weather,
the window saves us when we fly.

Inner inspirations

One way

One way
through valleys, over hills,
embedded in a pathless clime,
almost lost in colour frills,
required for the course of time.

One light
shines on repose; and flow
leads orientation soon astray
to directions targets throw;
a way-out just might leave the play.

Escape
wherever, over there;
to stay would squeeze the last reprieve,
if I poise I'll lose my chair;
dispersed, I use what's there to leave.

Inner inspirations

Horizons

Horizon is what we expect
beyond the last conceit;
the way to it we soon neglect
where earth and heaven meet.

This line of longings in a row,
so dense from far away,
gets blown just as dimensions grow,
unfolding spell's decay.

The point of view is much too near
to find a distant aim;
once found, allegedly, it's clear:
Look back to see the same.

Conjunctions, made of truth and dream,
may happen in our mind;
to feel horizons that don't seem,
our senses must be blind.

Inner inspirations

Swoosh of thoughts

In a swoosh of aimless thoughts,
crossing schedules they don't make,
flashes lead to thunderstorms,
let some sleepy seconds quake.

Startled up tranquillity,
puzzled, squirreling around,
finds again the swoosh to be,
gives my limbs to background's sound.

Yet I feel a difference,
atmospherics left behind,
formed by ether's prevalence,
later I make up my mind.

As the lightning disappears,
and the greying view turns back,
something evidently clears,
genesis draws white on black.

Freedom below skies

I fancy freedom
like dancing in the wind,
which means relying
on steps with no imprint.
I fancy flying
like jaunty melodies,
no need to sing them
but to inhale their ease.

I fancy drifting
below the clear, blue sky,
without directions
but letting courses try.
I fancy findings
sufficing for my life,
pretending nothing,
but letting me survive.

Inner inspirations

Path into consciousness

A path into my consciousness
is leading out of dark routines,
I'm pulled by thoughts of shininess
and meet myself away from scenes.

Experiences through my days
get mostly tidied night by night,
and dreams are just bad interplays,
don't understand but put things right.

Some time to ponder secretly
seems independent of my life,
and saving space consistently,
these seconds make my years survive.

There I may promenade a while
and see my light, confirming views;
this path is there, and without guile,
it lets me walk without life's shoes.

Inner inspirations

Japanese blossoms falling

Is it blossoms falling, white,
is it rather yet some snow,
can our time still hold us tight,
will it hurt the story, though?

Have we lived our love too long
lip on lip to fight the fall?
Heartbeat says it can't be wrong,
but in fear of homeland's call.

Memories in your eyes are clear,
pictures come and go astray,
through the black first tears appear
as companions for my way.

Can we really not retain
what a language can't retrieve?
Did we draw those dreams in vain,
which our big dream now must leave?

As I see these white flakes whirr
all around your straight, black hair,
I get lost in future's blur,
searching past days in despair.

Inner inspirations

Sights of mind

Idylls, full of lights and shadows,
howsoever I'm concerned,
keep much more in light on meadows,
and the darkness is not burnt.

I can feel my understanding
maybe just in black and white;
but when passing contrasts' blending,
it provides another sight.

Strength in calmness gives me power,
lets me do what it supplies,
not ideal and neither sour,
sensing landscapes' paint makes wise.

Short hand's tip

A fly on shorthand's tip,
and minutes, far away,
which burke each second's pip:
What's fleeting, what may stay?

The fly is doing itself up,
feels free since time gives scope,
and doesn't care about time's nub,
no reason to elope.

A fly on shorthand's tip
is riding seconds out;
but then one moment's flip
puts flight instincts to rout.

Dream on, my free ideas

Dream on, my free ideas,
I've never tried to make you real,
you simply ditch my fears
in emptiness with no appeal.

I hardly feel your urge.
Where has it gone, why do you hush?
In bondages I search
if anything caught up your rush.

My muse is still aware,
it's but my leisure, which is hit;
quite scared in darkness here,
and dreading loss of flash of wit.

Dream on, Ideas, I trust
and leave it all alone in peace;
dream on, my chase won't last -
to grant my spirit frank release.

Inner inspirations

Morning peace

Please, don't take my morning peace,
let me doze in dispositions;
waking turn by turn galls ease,
don't wake up my fading visions.

Live along! I won't catch up.
Leave me just a rest of twilight,
feeds my flesh, down to a nub,
speak the day, I'll stay in slack tide.

Dream away, into my dream,
say hello from nightly waste ground;
can't retard what thoughts may deem,
they have long since seized what I found.

Please don't take my morning peace,
sometime it will free my tears.
Will the final maw gulp these -
will I find some sleep that clears?

Inner inspirations

Facing

Self-will under autumn's roof,
strolling, nothing's left to prove,
high above old thoughts might flee,
won't sum up true ways to be.

I feel dopey but not downed,
pushing tiredness around,
yet peculiarly I'm led
by some spirit in my tread.

All that urged me now is pale,
somewhat yellowed in time's scale,
then a while befriends my mind,
and true memories may unwind.

As the year's remains soothe climes,
as the evening calms betimes,
there's not much I have achieved,
but I touch what I've believed.

Inner inspirations

Is it here?

Never playing with emotions,
now and here, where we feel close;
darkness shelters nightly notions,
and no nightmare left to pose.

We don't need to urge our senses
to unwind sensuality;
nearer than our skin condenses,
being near is meant to be.

Placid breath in whispering minding,
just a notion without will;
do not search what we are finding,
we confide what thoughts fulfil.

Have we simply found each other,
or will just recover soon
what no doubt might really bother,
trying to corrupt our boon?

I can't move this moment's musing,
comes towards me on its own,
and wherever you're now waiting,
time and space leave us alone.

Inner inspirations

Heart surgeon

She conquered finally my heart,
I didn't want it anyway;
before my pain ripped it apart,
she had befriended its decay.

Her face seemed much too young for me,
and yet it showed experience;
'you will not cheat my misery',
I told her with weak prevalence.

Her eyes, not sad but serious,
were asking, rather bright than shy;
'please leave me now delirious',
I said, 'and learn before you try'.

My age soon called me just a fool
when scorning inexperienced youth,
but as my conscience failed to rule,
I fell for her attempt to soothe.

I couldn't care 'cause she had won,
I woke up, feeling my release;
she saved my life, my pain had gone,
which just a heart surgeon could ease.

Inner inspirations

Smallest light

Wafted by a windy breeze,
with my longing for emotions;
where my breath can find some ease,
I'm without my gloomy notions.

There's no distant shine ahead,
offering itself as blender,
colours' shadows are not dead,
lasting truth makes dusk surrender.

In this quiet, lonely time
there's a brainwave of one power,
flowing freely, not to mime,
which makes otherwise hope sour.

And this smallest light appears,
in between the shades of history;
it is you, away from fears,
joining me, I keep your mystery.

Inner inspirations

Not just a simple smile

A simple smile,
from far away, so near,
and eyes beguile,
exotic, bright and clear.

An instant peak
of presence without word,
my knees get weak,
surrounded by the flirt.

No languages,
we've left them both at home,
our souls confess
their need of stealth to roam.

A distance stays,
a cultured little while
in notion sways:
It is no simple smile.

True wishes

I wish,
well, I miss a reason why
and what ... I need to try.
Foolish,
I, in fear of self-deceit,
I tell the wish in deed.

My head,
asking for the real content,
it hides how it is meant.
Forget
doubts, my conscience boldly says,
prevent yourself from stress.

I'm forced
by the tongs of strategy,
I miss my honesty.
Endorsed
by my feelings needs to feel,
that's what I wish for real.

Inner inspirations

Pounding will

Now I carry all away,
crazy, how it works my mind,
thoughts are riding on my prey
outward on a spiral's wind.

All at once I flee straight on,
and no backing stops my run,
feels like newborn since I've gone,
I escape all logic's stun.

Oh, so sensitive my fist -
here a gracious, open hand,
there a hammer at my wrist -
pounding will into its stand.

Future takes me by my speed,
comes towards my energy;
by no hurry haste could seed,
I get merged in what I see.

Nothing then can drag me down,
and my lot is out of range;
facing foresight I won't frown
with its noncommittal change.

Inner inspirations

The scribbler

A writer without readership
gave almost up on his ideas,
these lived in every written trip
while time ate paper without cheers.

He asked himself for passion's goal,
which couldn't sate, day in day out,
he felt quite healthy in his soul,
frustration made his illness proud.

But why, the desperate writer thought,
does everything take me away
from minds my spirit's always taught?
The world won't prove my own decay.

It only shows the big remain,
which does not spin around me, though;
I take my time it can't sustain,
I feed on what eats up the show.

Inner inspirations

Beyond the day

Not one soul destroys my peace
as my senses feel like blessed;
some are just about to cease,
others give their kids a nest.

Whirring days apart from calm
form no question for the night,
sending sparks throughout the balm;
I'm not sullen and not bright.

Light that sinks into the dark
is attending to my mind;
I'm alone in longing's park,
but replete with every kind.

Inner inspirations

City fright

May I listen to the rain
when outside the city streams;
can I find a sunny lane
where at nights the streetlight screams?

Will my routines leave some knack
as my natural will gets spoiled;
are there ways around a track,
which, by tight spots, won't be foiled?

Will my skin not fail to feel,
when the world jumps out of it;
is there time complaints can't steal,
time to sing and play a bit?

Must a word make way for talk,
since it goes unheard, alone;
can be silence with my walk,
or will death tear off its tone?

Inner inspirations

Remind my heart

I kiss my cup,
look at the clock.
Each second counts a day dream knock.
This minutes' crawl won't wake me up.

When do I start?
Too early yet
to bubble over to regret.
Another sip reminds my heart.

The mug is dead,
the clock stays round;
concerned, the hour has no sound.
Where is it from, where do I tread?

Along the clouds

Along the clouds my wishes disappear,
if more or less - with punch or with a beer;
I fall behind, and what I have is naught,
so what I am, is all that life has taught.

The moving skies above my silly mind
change everything that I cannot unwind;
what I can keep is only made to feel,
what I could give is mine and not for real.

Along the clouds I see a gap with light,
it shines between all future and my side;
a lack of shadowed continuity,
a blackout or a chance of destiny.

Inner inspirations

Lifetime bloom

Is a dream the end of life,
sleeping in our day time's bloom;
can a flower's kiss survive
when its cup's enclosed the gloom?

May tomorrow set it free
to expose it to the sun;
how can wishes trust to be
still a part of partial fun?

Change a bit the point of view,
darkness is a fake inside,
find the stem, belonging to,
leads to roots from senses' light.

My inner self

I'm bottled up close to his cage,
he binds me to his misery;
who am I to respect this mage,
pretends to be quite brotherly.

He roams my curious attempts,
however I'm affectionate;
I look at him as he pre-empts
my try to cage my searching fate.

Our pairs of eyes at once are one,
and truly I'm not here but there;
I keep the cage, while he has gone,
shouts neener-neener! anywhere.

Inner inspirations

Out of my house

Just one light that hits the street,
from a house there on its own,
what I feel it cannot meet,
and the moon shines on alone.

There's a wandering silhouette
by the lit up window pane,
cannot find a peaceful bed,
longing for some rest in vain.

Darkness otherwise begirds
windows, garden and a gate.
Where's that life no shadow hurts,
life my conscience likes to state?

Evenings take me there to roam,
no idea about the spell,
but my dream calls it 'my home',
knows much more, which truth can't tell.

And I see our years go by,
understanding we behold,
sun and moon may testify,
still I'm left out in the cold.

Now I'm finished for tonight,
and my fate feels somehow sealed,
then your voice calls through that light:
Wake up darling, you are healed.

Inner inspirations

Beside you

Keeping silence by your side,
ask myself for words you said,
where I go they are my guide,
now beyond the time we had.

In the forest I am free
to experience what I feel;
in my face from you and me
tranquil smiles make memories real.

By the glade you fade away,
under Sunday's sunny beams;
oddly peaceful to their play
distant bells attend my dreams.

Under bridges

There, where I don't know my life,
without struggle, without ease,
under bridges I'll survive,
taking jags to fantasies.

'Cause my future seems too cold,
gave rehashed security;
pass my present to unfold
freedom solitarily.

When my shadow wakes up then,
no more light keeps it at bay;
I may blindly leave its ban
since that light must go each day.

Get lost with me

Can you hear me,
I believe it has been calmly happening,
let us try to find and see,
it will come true, intuiting.

Let your words flow,
what you say is meant to feed intimacy,
which I feel without to know
where we - from here and there - will flee.

Look here and stay,
there is aimless time enough to live along;
in new light the shadows play,
get lost with me as we are strong.

Bluish night

Bluish haze, which shrouds the night,
asphalt cuts me out of sleep,
queerly clear, I roam this sight,
and the truth beyond seems deep.

There I go to find the dawn,
blue like pale, might bring no change.
What could free me from my yawn,
which is out of choice's range?

Streets behind me, land ahead,
morning sun looks kind of spent.
Will I wake up where I tread,
may the blue skies know the end?

Inner inspirations

Window *at* the wall

There's a window *at* the wall,
I've been waiting here so long,
outside's nothing that could call,
every movement seems so wrong.

From beyond, that frozen light,
doesn't hit me as I look,
seems to shine, but isn't bright,
try to catch but cannot hook.

As I search my shadowed room
for a soul that suits my flesh,
I feel heartbeats: Boom! by Boom!
Rising fears that I can't dash.

I've just tried to prove good will,
daily madly drilled to crawl;
what my longing can't fulfil,
is that picture at the wall.

Repatriation

A pain that has been lasting long
sits deep in my initial heart,
in hazy notion getting strong,
tears chains around my soul apart.

There I got lost, in days of old,
forgotten throughout coming past;
my courage now tries to unfold
what waits for me - what waits to last.

The images guide all my feel,
and silence shivers in a breeze,
makes ancient voices almost real,
I seem familiar with this ease.

And faces follow soon their words,
now watching my reverse comeback,
I am where my origin hurts,
so lost in time, but on my track.

Again I live it all around,
but knowing not to go too far;
my own continuum I've found
as satellite of bloodline's star.

I need to go, life has its right,
'to be' means 'merciless today',
it leaves me in its instant light,
I'm still alone but know my way.

Inner inspirations

In memories

I'm lying in my memories
of moments beyond time and place,
embedded in so youthful leaves.
And lights between a whispering tune
are moved by a familiar breeze
while plying with my blinking face.

I cannot feel the winter yet,
and nor the summer to grow up;
deigns youngsters love struck jauntiness
I wish I won't have to regret.

My goose bumps make me fancy this,
no rampant senses claim my mind
to waste the secret that I feel;
a little water, just near by,
is gurgling softly, tones of bliss,
I'm one with it in moment's find.

Is someone there who knows me here?
No, it's just me who tempts the scene,
not getting used to it too much,
'cause what I leave returns somewhere.

Inner inspirations

Home bound

All I miss ...

... the path
I stumbled in the end;
the road
that took me over there;
the sea
that washed me up onshore;
the bank
that tempted me to flee.

All my bliss ...

... my walk,
yet weak but with new trend;
my run
that lifts my inner sphere;
the stream
to cool my mental sore;
the land,
my country touches me.

Inner inspirations

An undiscovered land

As little point, I'm floating, free,
I'm watching worlds surrounding me,
there's nothing that prevents my view,
gets dipped in water without clue.

The waves are dancing all along,
my boat is easily among,
a teasing little splash with fizz
jumps into it with cheekiness.

I follow to my bijou's rim,
and reaching out for water's vim,
I roam its undiscovered land,
my presence takes me by its hand.

I move along on fortune's course,
its peacefulness is my resource;
I realise that endless space
when never leaving, place by place.

Inner inspirations

I-Instance

It sits so deep,
indefinitely deep
so much too deep,
and almost beyond any doubt;
it had to sleep,
a deadly too long sleep,
a long lost sleep
no dream could be about.

What is its aim,
its claimed, ambitious aim,
evading aim,
to let its conscience search?
It took my name,
no matter how to name,
to need no name,
which just it self can urge.

Who'll stay off me,
in memory of me -
of only me -
when all this question will be gone?
Just wait, and see
it says, I'll see;
what's yours to see,
another one brings on.

Inner inspirations

Way to salvation

Solid ways don't find salvation,
only water meets the light;
brightest heavens show sensation,
shadows level all my sight.

Yet I fear my own old footsteps,
once too far, they'll surely sink;
if I follow, shunning time traps,
I will float from brink to brink.

When I've learned to trust the water,
I can feel the loss of weight;
don't need words as self supporter
since the whisper fish's my guide.

A tiny dream

My tiny dream,
now you are here,
quite blowsed by wild reality,
and not yet liking to be stroked,
my tiny dream,
I'm in your sphere.

You are awake
and don't know why,
you don't believe what you can see,
but look it's easily evoked,
oh, stay awake,
so we can fly.

Inner inspirations

Hand in hand

Once I looked into a soul
that confided in my face,
occupied my spirit's place,
I felt strange in stranger's role.

I was split, from heart to heart,
then tripartite by a pain:
public vanity in vain
versus loneliness apart.

In between I found no rest,
watched that soul's disunity,
suffering of how to be,
whoop and dying in my chest.

Finally I was alone
in myself, and quite distraught;
but a hand that mine had caught
found some crutch as trust had grown.

Inner inspirations

After all I am

And after all, I am what I have been,
on my experienced track throughout the search,
just step by step through countries I have seen,
I was a fool, well stalled by fortune's urge.

What was that urge, I ask myself today.
A tool to flee out of my inner hope?
I longed in deed for targets without way,
the natives' view was nothing I could cope.

Soon welcomed here, soon grounded anywhere,
but never left existence to a wraith;
I was content, that's what my mouth made clear,
but friendship failed in terms of wordless faith.

I carried on to find what no one tells
and sent my aims into my lonely lot;
there was no chance to set them somewhere else,
can't separate my dreams from what I've got.

Inner inspirations

My final love

My final love, yet far away
beyond my inner crutch,
I wish I were where we could stay,
I thought of it too much.

I want to keep it in my heart,
just swaying, mind to mind,
but candle dreams light just my part,
make inner mirrors blind.

I live on longing night by night,
which drives my feelings mad,
and captured by my one way sight,
I'm all I've ever had.

And yet my hoping, living lie
has occupied all dreams,
but sometime they will learn to fly
and feed what truth redeems.

Inner inspirations

Three ways

Three ways I need to go now, three:
ahead, to find the present age,
and back to check its current stage,
into myself from where to be.

One target should be there, just one,
made of reality by now,
preceding future to show how,
to focus progress that has gone.

Much time I want to take along,
which leads to opportunities,
the aim so close, no way to cease,
and rules not getting guidelines wrong.

Different home land

Homeland, you seem different now,
after years of emigration,
living faithlessly no nation
northbound, southbound, don't know how.

Times beforehand promised much,
teasing me with gold by cupper,
a betraying, weathering upper,
sepia warps new sorrows' touch.

Homeland, help me find my roots,
broke away from homeless yearning,
missing past, and no more learning,
don't show future, sing old moods.

Inner inspirations

Scent of time

My breath is longing for that scent,
was brought by winds from sea and land.
Where has it gone or blown away,
by storms abducted, led astray?

From places far away it told
of spirit of adventure's gold;
I took it on to dig it out,
it let me live and made me proud.

The surfeit of the world was mine,
and love and money got in line,
and so just longing stayed to keep,
yet it got old and somehow cheap.

Still it is smelling of it here,
I take a breath and waste a tear,
and from afar it comes again,
but missing times of youthful ken.

Inner inspirations

Another poem for my heart

Another poem I will give
and then I'll go to sleep, my heart;
I won't forsake you since we live,
in weal and woe we share each part.

I write it down in every line
that I have lived my world with you;
it's tailor-made for our time,
will later timelessly come true.

It is fool's gold around my truth,
I blind that sheen with my ideas,
and rhyme by rhyme they're gaining youth,
they let me go to leave my fears.

Now, come, my heart, I'd like to dance,
lets cling to whirling, final words;
the full stop's set to take the chance,
and where we go no heartache hurts.

~ ~ ~